The Perfect Gift

A collection of motivational, humorous and spiritual poetry, with an interactive poetry writing competition!

By

Amanda Anderson.

Independently Published by CKB Press
13 Shannon Cove, Dromod,
Co. Leitrim, Republic of Ireland
Email: info@ckbpress.com
Website: www.ckbpress.com

First Edition

ISBN: 978-1-914133-15-2

Dedication

I would like to dedicate this book to the following people:

Firstly; to my late grandmother, Joan Smith, for all the stories that she read to me as a small child, and for her endless encouragement and patience, when teaching me to read.

The foundations laid in those early days, have always supported me well.

Secondly; to my son Rhys, who shares my love of the English language, and who appreciates (like no other), the distinctive aroma and 'feel' of a printed book.

Also; to my niece Amy, in acknowledgment of our treasured conversations, on many things.

To my friends; Deb, Lesley and Dee, with whom I also, share Spiritual perspectives.

Finally; to my husband Leighton, sister Lucy, RF Susie, and extended family & friends, who support and cheer me on.

Thank you.

Acknowledgements

I would also like to gratefully acknowledge the following people:

Beth Baldwin; Thank you for your generosity of spirit, in helping me to gain clarity and focus.

Holding space for others, truly is 'The Perfect Gift'.

Karen Brown; (www.coachkarenbrown.com) for her willingness to inspire and support. "It is no coincidence that we find the perfect people, at the perfect time". Thank you for being this person.

Amanda Tooke; (www.theangelmystic.co.uk) for sharing her knowledge and inspiration, and also to all the other members of 'Abundance Club' group, who have become special friends.

Sybil Fowler; Thank you for the introduction to the Facebook group "Inspirational Women of the World" (founded by Dawn Evans and Tracey Marie Smolinski).

(This is a collective of truly, inspirational women, and features in the poem "Motivational Monday").

Contents

Meet the Author:

Amanda Anderson is a Spiritual, inspirational, humorous, and motivational poet.

Rhyming verse has always been her passion-ever since as a young child, she discovered the thrill of 'cat, rat and mat'.

This is her first Poetry collection, and features a combination of humorous, inspirational and motivational verse, with a little 'twist' at the end of the book.

She has also published an extensive range of Journals, in the hopes of encouraging others to write-including Dream & Gratitude Journals, in the Sparkle Me Spiritual series.

(www.sparkle-me-spiritual.com)

There is also a 'My Friends' series of journals.

These are all available on Amazon.

Amanda is married, with a son and lives in Cardiff, South Wales. UK.

Sparkle
Me
Spiritual

Sparkle Me Spiritual

'Sparkle me Spiritual'...What could that mean?
I guess, it's to 'drench one, in things yet unseen'.
My journey's progressing, o'er such a long time-
Much longer, than ever could share, within rhyme.

I started my life, knowing just black and white-
Until up popped grey, which adjusted my sight.
What I always thought... No wait...! Always knew!
Now, turns out not to be, totally true!

Where does 'faith' come from, in absence of proof?
(The Tooth Fairy/Santa Claus, up on the roof.)
As children, we feel into mystery and charm-
As adults, experience 'mystic disarm'.

Do we focus too much, on the concrete and ground?
(Oblivious, to Spiritual pointers around.)
Do you talk to your Angels, when feathers appear?
Do you ask them for help to make blurred become clear?

Contd.

Sparkle Me Spiritual

Does with you lie knowing? A calling, so strong?
A linking, to something far greater, belong?
(than life on this planet), which one day, will end.
Do you hold belief, that your soul will transcend?

We all choose our programme-We wake to new day;
We each have free will, to re-route errant way.
Don't wait 'til tomorrow, to start patterns new-
Find, and invest in the Spiritual you!

What are you waiting for?

Is there a passion, that burns to your core?
A yearning, to better your lot?
Is there a whisper, you just can't ignore?
A dream, that will not, be forgot?
What does your heart say? Be still-'go within'-
Listen to seek clarity.
To walk away now, would be surely, a sin-
Where lies your disparity?
The life you're now living- is it truly aligned,
to all that's authentically you?
Or, do you end days, feeling somewhat maligned,
by things which you find, you must do?
Does your soul bounce with joy, at the start of a day?
Do you leap out of slumber excited?
Or has it become, just 'familiar' way?
Then your path, really now must be righted!

Contd.

What are you waiting for?

'It's not a rehearsal', (the 'sayings' remind)-
Unfulfilled time will be lost.
It's 'prime' to unshackle, those grim chains that bind-
The price comes, at too high a cost.
It's time now to wise-up, to plot your new course-
Dispense with façade, and untrue.
Do not live a second more, with the remorse,
of a life, that feels alien to you.
If your passion is writing, then take up your pen-
If it's music, let this fill your heart!
Decide when you sleep tonight, that your 'Amen',
will herald tomorrow's new start.
We all have 'two' lives- it's important to note,
that the second one, can only start-
Once we realize, that we do, only have one-
Which dawns, when we follow our heart.

Your order has been received

Have you, ever had a feeling firm,
of something, meant to be?
You didn't know how it would come-
Just that you'd wait and see!

You felt it, in your deepest soul-
You saw it, clear and bright-
You heard it, with excited ears-
Held vision, clear in sight.

Each day, the feeling deepens-
Drawing closer, not a doubt!
Your deeper, inner knowing says:
"It's soon to come about".

Excitement builds...You want to dance-
A fountain, bubbling strong-
You feel the tingle on your skin-
You know it won't be long!

Contd.

Your order has been received

You set your focus, on this prize...
You've lived it, (in your heart)-
You know, that it's your destiny-
Of your life- it's a part!

Your energy, was clear aligned-
Your order placed, with action...
Then 'it' arrived, in perfect time-
'Care of' LAW OF ATTRACTION.

The jewellery box

I own, a quite old jewellery box,
made from dark green leather.
It doesn't look its shiny best-
(has seen some stormy weather.)

It lived its life, for many years,
as friend, to my late mother.
(Standing by a turquoise one,
gifted by my brother.)

It struck me, that this treasure trove,
is pretty much, like life-
It holds a hoard of trinkets-
Worn as child, as girl, or wife.

Every day, we get to choose,
a piece that will adorn-
Accompaniment, to all events,
we celebrate or mourn.

Contd.

The jewellery box.

Some days, we want to shout out loud-
Flamboyant colours boast-
Then other days, our favourite pearls;
(The ones, we love the most.)

We may feel shiny, glistening-
Like Silver, sparkling bright;
On other days, we favour jet-
The darkness, of the night.

On sunny days-it's coloured beads,
which vibrancy, convey-
The joy, we radiate in our life;
The optimistic way!

The beauty is, that every day,
we can, select anew.
Make it your priority,
to choose, what best, suits you.

This was the handwritten copy that we found...

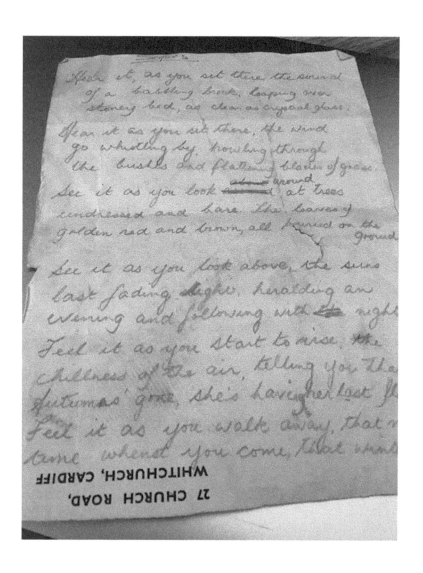

Introduction to "Senses"...

The following poem "Senses", was written by my mother, Hilary Patricia Teague in the 1960's.

She passed away in 2018, and when we were clearing her house, we came across this little piece of treasure.

Although not written strictly in rhyming couplets, this poem, simply and beautifully, reflects her appreciation of Mother Nature, and the Seasons.

One of the songs that we played at her funeral was "All my Life's a Circle" by 'The New Seekers'.

Finding this poem, felt like validation that this was an appropriate choice.

All things are cyclical.

Amanda. X

Senses

Hear it… as you sit there, the sound of babbling brook;
Leaping over stony bed, as clear as crystal glass.
Hear it …as you sit there, the wind a' whistling by;
Howling through the bushes and flattening blades of grass.

See it… as you look around, at trees undressed in sight;
Their leaves of golden red and brown, all buried on the ground.
See it… as you look above, the sun's last fading light;
Heralding an evening, and followed, by night around.

Feel it… as you start to rise- the chillness of the air;
Telling you that Autumn's gone. (she's having her last flare).
Feel it… as you walk away- that next time, when you come;
That winter will give rise to this, and yet, be robbing some.

Turn not- but picture in your mind what nature will have done;
Encased this scene in snowy white-That stark, bare trees will sparkle bright;
And rise to show their lacy cobwebs, 'gainst the greyness of night.
The brook be stilled, babble on no more but lay there, icy-bright.

Contd.

Senses

Walk slowly now, on up the hill, pull cloak around, to feel no chill.

Turn not around, though you feel you might, to behold once more, this magical sight.

Feel it deep within your heart, embed it in your mind-

That next time you return to this, remember what you find.

Then, when you turn away to go, and make an uphill start-

That after this, the bells will ring,

and colour will fill the world again;

To pay tribute, to the treasure of the Spring.

Hilary Patricia Teague 1945-2018

They are there

Do you believe in Angels?
Have you felt their guiding love?
Or are you yet, to sense them?
(Your 'A team' 'up above.')

Had you asked me this 5 years ago-
A smile you would have raised-
But life plays out, in quite strange ways-
My perspective; 'reappraised'!

We all have Angels, (yes, you too!)-
Regardless of belief.
They're there to help with all in life,
(In happy times, and grief.)

Around not just for tough times,
but in celebrations too.
Invite them to your party-
Let them sit awhile, with you.

Contd.

They are there

Feel their tickle on your face-
See 'calling cards' around;
The unexpected feather-
Shiny penny, on the ground.

The butterfly, that flutters by-
Perhaps it ventures near;
These common signs, that Angels bring,
to tell you, that they're here.

Have you, ever seen a sparkle,
out the corner of your eye?
(which summons your attention-
thinking, something's passing by.)

You turn to look, and with surprise-
There's nothing there to see!
You end up, saying to yourself;
"Ah well... must just be me"!

loA

You may well, have heard of it- what could this be?
A system of sending, what I want, to me?
We know that there's Etsy, and Amazon Prime,
(They also 'deliver', in fairly prompt time.)

What then, you may ask, is so special 'bout this?
An 'order' that's placed, with a feeling of bliss.
You don't need to think, of delivery date;
But trust that it's coming- may be a short wait.

What is there to do, whilst awaiting arrival?
Well... each day 'engage in emotion revival'.
Just FEEL into what it is, that you now seek,
It may arrive next month, today, or next week.

It's all about energy, and your vibration!
You mustn't let thoughts, become blobs of stagnation.
You must hold your focus, on all 'highest good'-
Trust that it's working out, just as it should.

Contd.

loA

It sounds a bit strange, but as wise folk will know-
'Thoughts become things', so let energy flow;
to all that is in you, that you may desire-
The inextinguishable, bright-burning fire.

Today you create, what tomorrow will bring.
Send out your request, for this wonderful thing.
Be grateful for what you have, now in the day-
Then, look out for so much more heading your way!

If it can be imagined, and held in belief-
You must not let doubt, be your energy thief.
Don't limit your thoughts or keep hope in confinement-
Hold your vibration, in constant alignment.

It's there for the asking, and please never doubt,
that the Universe listens- you never need shout!
You focus your dream, taking inspired action-
Awaiting delivery, by Law of Attraction.

Introduction to 'Motivational Monday'

This poem was written for a Facebook group, to which I am proud to belong.

The intention, of this group, is for women to come together, to support, uplift, and motivate one another.

The group is called Inspirational Women of the World.

(IWOW).

Motivational Monday

"Motivational Monday";

Let the upbeat vibes, now flow!

A chance for us, some words to say,

which may help others grow.

We've joined in commune, in a group-

To support, uplift and praise;

Like a mug of soul food, (chicken soup),

which sustains, on chilly days.

We all get times, which try us sore-

Doubts, which leave us low-

When, 'creative juice' seeps out the door,

and there's nowhere, left to go.

When faith is stretched, and faltering,

by funds, a bit depleted-

Our mind, we must get altering,

to stop this being repeated!

Contd.

Motivational Monday

"Thoughts become things", the saying claims-

We attract, that on which, we dwell-

So today, and each day, set firmly your aims,

that all things, are going to be well.

Think back, to when you first started out-

'Felt the fear', but still, jumped right in!

Do not 'buy in', to gloom, loss or doubt-

Re-kindle your fire within.

You know the one- that powerful voice-

Which bellowed at you, that you COULD!

The one, which drove, all of your positive choice-

Your instinct, that this, will be good!

So today, be mindful of what you think-

Embrace the 'Law of Attraction';

Don't let your self-worth, or passion sink-

Instead, take inspired action!

Contd.

GRATITUDE
TURNS WHAT
-WE-
Have
INTO
Enough

Motivational Monday

See what you do have, with wide, honest eyes-

'Go within' and ask the questions.

Keep going girl! Claim that prize!...

List your gratitude-need some suggestions?

How about, the sunny day?

The coffee, in your cup?

The moon, which lights your night-time way?

The arrow? (Which way is up?)

The people, who have shaped your life?

(The ones, who love and care.)

The saviours, when in times of strife,

you know- are always there.

Then there's you, yes, wonderful you!

(Your very own, best friend.)

The one, who'll always get you through-

On whom, you can depend.

Contd.

Motivational Monday

Pick up your sword and feel your power-

Have faith that you'll come through!

Don't waste another precious hour,

not trying something new.

Are you 'glass half empty', or 'glass half-full'?

Will you venture, outside the box?

Are you steadfast and mighty, as a bull?

Or resourceful, as an Urban fox?

You CAN do, and you MUST do!

Remember- you've come so far-

If change is called for, then start anew-

Try always, to raise your own bar.

Keep focused, keep calm, and keep moving ahead-

Small steps, or gigantic leap.

If you get a bit weary, then jump into bed-

Don't ever dismiss 'power of sleep'.

Contd.

I
CAN
and
I
will.
Watch
me

Motivational Monday

Keep your momentum, and ongoing motion…

Your story is written by you!

View challenges, as 'inspirational lotion',

which helps 'lubricate', progress new!

You're awesome…you've got this-you're strong, and you're wise,

Just trust, that you're on the right track.

Look straight ahead, with your confident eyes-

That the Universe, HAS got your back!

On days, when it feels, like a struggle uphill-

When there's no help, to carry your load-

Shout loud, from the rooftops, "I can, and I will"

Then, pick up your pace, on life's road.

Try often to think not, "Now what can I take"?

But flip it, to 'What can I give"?

Then 'give of yourself', just for true, giving sake-

As this, is the best way, to live.

Mothering Sunday 2020

There is a fixed tradition,
that on a certain day-
We all buy gifts, and greetings cards,
with meaning to convey.

It is, to honour 'mums' (and like),
who've nurtured, and supported-
Whose care of us is steadfast,
and whose love, is never thwarted.

Today though, feels quite different-
a disruptive beast's at war,
(with humanity, as we know it)-
it's ripping out our floor.

Our people are in fear;
Our infrastructure swaying;
Our Commerce fractures daily,
and our children, are not playing.

Contd.

Mothering Sunday 2020

"The best of times, the worst of times,"
is now, for the Collective-
We're all at risk, from Covid threat,
-it truly, ain't selective!

Our world continues to evolve,
great riches we've attained,
raining from our ears,
(a tribute, to the left-brained).

So why, (we plea), has this happened?
Why have things got so grim?
What have we done, to deserve such blows?
Do the answers lie, maybe within?

Our scientists, speak complex words,
as to how this came about-
Our Medics battle bravely…
of this-let be no doubt.

Contd.

Mothering Sunday 2020

But what may be the other side?
(The lessons we've not learned.)
Taken all for granted,
abused privilege, we once earned.

Are we now being called, to stop/reset?
Rethink our errant ways?
Is there light, at end of tunnel?
Or close, to "End of Days"?

On this day, we honour those, who've helped,
to raise us higher-
Let's not forget, our Mother Earth-
Give thanks, to Planet GAIA.

Carpe Diem

Life's rich dance.

There comes a time, of 'time no more'-
Where, days no longer, knock your door.
In the meantime, take your chance-
To fully sway, in life's rich dance.

Seize your moment- fix your crown;
Don't let others, bring you down.
Speak your truth, and live your passion;
Wear your quirky, mixed-up fashion.

Love your tribe, embrace your mission;
Strive, to reach your core ambition.
Drink the wine, (if that's your thing).
Do, what makes your glad heart sing!

Be brave, be bold, but humble too-
Then live your life, as 'truly you'.
'Carpe Diem' every day-
In your special, unique way.

FORGIVENESS DOES NOT
change the past,
BUT IT DOES ENLARGE
the future

Forgiveness

When somebody wrongs you,
it's easy then to feel-
A sense, of strong injustice,
at this spoke, placed in your wheel.

We take things sadly, to our heart,
and store, them tight within.
This, is always, without doubt,
an example, of 'no win'.

Why did they have to hurt me?
Betray, or cause me harm?
Why did they spoil my default setting?
(peace, and inner calm.)

I, so didn't deserve that-
I really did, no wrong;
So why does this, unwanted feeling,
to me, now, belong?

Contd.

Forgiveness

I'm sad, and I'm angry...
unsettled, quite enraged;
through the wrong, that happened-
that the 'other person', staged!

It wasn't my fault- honestly!
- no small part, did I play.
Oh, how I wish, this feeling,
would now, swiftly, go away.

We've argued, we've fought,
and we've now arrived, right here;
A resolution isn't coming-
that's becoming clear!

We're both holding on, to
our own, firm sense of 'right';
Neither feels responsible,
for, this unpleasant fight.

Contd.

forgive
them anyway

Forgiveness

We will not be persuaded,
that we too, had played a role-
In destruction, of the mutual peace,
the growling beast, then stole.

There's seems no place to go,
when you willfully, won't see-
That there always, will be
two sides, of responsibility.

Could you maybe have looked,
at the other one's side?
Perhaps, just a tiny bit harder,
have tried?

To have made some allowance,
for human transgression?
Come on now- own up!
Let's hear your confession.

Contd.

THE FIRST TO APOLOGIZE
is the
BRAVEST
THE FIRST TO FORGIVE
is the
STRONGEST
THE FIRST TO FORGET
is the
HAPPIEST

Forgiveness

There'll always be two sides,
for actions uncouth-
There's your side, and their side-
and then, there's the truth.

Please stop for a moment,
and replay the scene;
Can you truly, not see,
what your part, may have been?

When all has been said,
and the issue been aired;
It's time, for the matter,
to then, be repaired.

Do not now waste precious time,
harbouring hate-
Resolve, and rebuild this,
before it's too late.

My passion

Flowers are my passion...
and plants- I love them too;
They make me smile- they lift my soul;
Do they do this, for you?

Lavender... I scent you;
Gentle fragrance calms the mind.
Fuschia... I just cannot wait,
for your pink bells, to find.

Lobelia... tiny plant of cluster,
blue, or pink, or white;
When huddled close together;
what a pure, inspiring sight.

Geranium... you fine display,
with shocks of vibrancy.
Frilly flowers of Hollyhock,
with stalk, far-reaching me.

Contd.

My passion

Magnolia and Begonia,
reflecting golden light;
I could not, more adore you,
even try hard, as I might.

Pansy, you just make me feel,
you're smiling just for me;
Your faces, so much cuter,
than the cutest face, could be.

Petunia- you can't disappoint-
You always, make the show!
(with your vibrant, splash of colour...
happy flower bells, you grow.)

Verbena... you are just so sweet;
your tiny, fairy kiss.
I do, so mourn, the Summer's fade-
Your performance, I will miss.

Contd.

My passion

I get you, Busy Lizzies…
you just cannot pause a while;
You just keep going, endlessly,
and always, make me smile.

Passionflower, Clematis,
Sweet pea, and Poppy too…
My garden's blessed, when you show up,
in all your glorious hue.

So many friends- I love you all!
I've roll-called, but, a few.
You light my life, on each new day-
If-you only knew!

But one last call, I have to give,
to Agapantha blue-
With, starry firework clusters,
I, forever will, love you.

Love from The Universe x

Hey you! What's that big sad face?
What's weighing on your soul?
You need to find your happy place,
to take you back, to whole.

Do you think, that no-one cares?
You trundle on alone?
Facing each day, unawares,
Your life-in monotone.

Where'd you lose your sparkling flame?
(That twinkle, in your eye?)
Was it bearing others blame-
The cold, despondent sigh?

Were there just, too many wars,
which sunk your spirit low?
Ever facing, firm-closed doors,
with nowhere, left to go?

Contd.

Love from The Universe x

Do you sometimes sit and think;
"Well, where do I belong?"
To hear your motivation sink!
(It's playing that old song.)

"I'll never make it, find my Dharma-
I matter not, to one.
Just staying, living out my Karma?
But, never feel the sun?"

If this is you, then stop this now-
Whatever's gone before...
It's time, to bless the here and now-
Set sail, to different shore.

You're not alone, I'm by your side
Your hand, I'm holding tight.
I'll journey with you, on your ride-
I'll help you, find your light.

Contd.

Love from The Universe x

Do not stop trying! Look anew!
There's other way to thrive!
Who thought, that when the acorn grew, an Oak tree,
would arrive?

If it feels too hard, your pathway blocked,
with problems in each pace;
Never think, ALL doors are locked-
Just move, another space.

Keep going forward, hold the thought,
that this too, soon shall pass.
If times are feeling, "oh so fraught"-
Adjust your looking glass.

See the lesson in ALL things-
You've come to learn and grow.
Find the gift that challenge brings-
I've got your back, you know.

Contd.

Love from The Universe x

I won't desert you- leave your track,
or ever, not be there-
I may, at times, step gently back,
to let you, find your flair.

But, know that you are treasured;
My faith in you, is cast.
My love for you, unmeasured;
For eternity, will last.

Decisions

I'd love to write a poem, but,
I don't know where to start!
(There's obviously, a knack,
to penning rhyming form of art.)

What is there to write about?
(Uncertain, what I know.)
Where do I start, (and, once on track)
how does the process go?

I just can't get it going-
What on earth's my opening line?
I'm certain, if I just find this,
the rest will flow, just fine.

Shall I talk of love, or fluffy clouds?
Lonely daffodils?
Of balmy, summer evenings?
Of mist-draped, far-off hills?

Contd.

Decisions

Of beauty, or of heartbreak, or,
the meaning of this life?
Of heartfelt bliss, which makes you glow?
Or endless, soul felt strife?

What happens if I get there?
If I manage to create?
Will anybody read it?
Think it's dreadful? Think it's great?

Could I bring, a momentary smile,
to someone's downturned lips,
by waxing/waning lyrical,
of grand, historic ships?

Or, painting by Picasso? Monet?
...maybe, Vince Van Gogh?
Or 'Cuisine Haute', with beefy theme?
(Wellington/Stroganoff.)

Contd.

Decisions

Perhaps, I'll write of Spiritual things,
which comfort, and inspire...
that offer words to motivate,
and raise vibration, higher.

Oh goodness me, it really feels, like
this will be, quite hard;
But I'll keep on trying, in my quest,
to wear, the cloak of bard!

Time to fly

My dear...I have to tell you-
as you really, need to know;
You did not come, to play it small-
You planted here, to grow.

You aren't cut out for ordinary-
To never, stake your claim;
To not show up, as your truest self-
You must, make this your aim.

You know you hold the power-
Let that Superwoman fly!
There will never be, a better time,
to soar, above your sky.

Birdsong

Sing up guys! It's been too long,
since we heard, your glorious song.
The air rings true-such clarity!
Sound and nature...parity.

The early dawn is punctuated-
Traditional 'chorus' re-instated.
The thrush, the sparrow, pigeon, dove...
All sing proud, with joy, with love.

Our sky is light, chemtrails no more-
A better option- that's for sure!
Pollution's better-emissions lower;
Nature's now, regaining power.

Sing up guys! Sing from your heart!
Your song now speaks, of brand, new start.
We hope, that Earth's recalibrating;
Let's hear, your sweet song, celebrating.

Rainforest

Come take a stroll, through the rainforest tropical-
Hear the sweet, birdsong clear!
'Deforestation'-now that, is so topical...
Robbing Earth, of its trees, held dear.

We need, and we want, the biodiversity;
The mammals, the plants, and the birds.
The ones, who fight now, against such adversity;
Those, who no longer, have herds.

We need the rain! We don't want drought;
Losing fight 'gainst Climate change.
It's now, you really need to shout!
(Or, our world, will look so strange.)

Imagine a planet, devoid of its greenery-
With no birdsong, crickets or fish.
Our blank canvas- stripped, of its glorious scenery-
How can this, be anyone's wish?

E-l-a-s-t-i-c

Ain't elastic just fantastic?
Think what it can do!
It holds secure, and keep things safe-
And, gives things life anew.

It's greatest perk, (at least for me)-
Is how, it makes things grow!
(It adds some inches, at a push)-
It's versatile, you know!

The boon for most-it has to be,
if eating a large dinner...
Elastic waistband saves the day, and
makes you feel, much thinner!

Without it- just think where we'd be-
with undies 'on the floor'!
Our socks, would not stay up our legs-
Not great for shoes, for sure!

Contd.

E-la-s-t-i-c

Then, what about spring onions?
How would they stay together?
They like to hang out, in a bunch,
(as 'bestest' friends, forever.)

Most important, is the mail,
the 'Postie' brings each day;
Without a band, to keep them safe-
Our letters, may well, stray!

And, just before I do forget-
You put it on your finger...
To help remind you, what you need,
and help the memory linger!

So next time, that you go to throw,
a 'Lacky band away...
Just think of all it does for you-
And save, for future day!

Inspirational

What, is inspirational?
(Good question you may ask.)
Is it, one who finds,
a novel way, to, face a task?

Someone, who strives hard,
and long, at University?
Or struggles through, each day of life,
against adversity?

Is it one, who spends their time,
just trying, to, 'buck the trend'?
Or is it one, who knows
the weight, of being a true friend?

A parent, who has found themselves,
a new, lone path to travel?
When, all they had, and all they loved,
had started, to unravel.

Contd.

Inspirational

The one, who gives so freely,
of their energy, and time?
(Holding space for others-
wrapping safe, in arms sublime.)

Is it, one who's lost their sight,
to then, help others see?
The mother, who has lost her child,
and battles, just 'to be'?

Could it be, the soldier-brave-
Their Country to defend?
(Who war, has rendered broken,
with a mind, that cannot mend).

Is it the child, whose life was struck?
(when they saw their father die.)
Then, (in his memory), grew up strong,
and spread their wings, to fly?

Contd.

Inspirational

How about, the one who feeds
the homeless, and the poor?
(Who, gives from little that they have,
and offers 'open door'.)

Is it one, who's changed the world,
by brilliant invention?
A member of Community,
who lives, by good intention?

The nurse, whose shift's long-ended,
but whose heart, tells her to stay,
to hold the grateful, hand
of one, whose life, now, ebbs away?

All above, (and many more),
inspire me, every day.
With souls as these, who give so much,
our world, will find, its way.

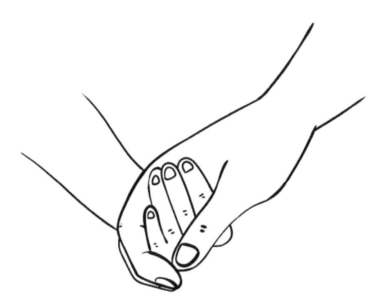

5D

Use your words to uplift others-
Praise and motivate.
Take up your pen, and get to work-
In others...celebrate!

Listen with ears, feel with soul;
Don't let this, be selective.
We join as one, to elevate,
our awakening, Collective.

Seek out those, who need support;
Send love, to one and all.
Speak only, words of kindness-
Let there be, no judgement call.

There's change afoot, as never known-
You're playing out your Karma.

Compassion, love & gratitude-
In this, you'll find your Dharma.

Lesson or Blessing

At times when you feel, that you can take, no more-
Your hope, and your confidence walked out the door;
This is the time, to stop fighting so hard;
Just take a moment, to let down your guard.

Step back from the issues, removed tainted glasses.
Trust in your knowing, that 'everything passes'.
There will be a way, and progress will ensue;
Trust that there's better times, coming for you!

Life is a series of twists, tugs and turns-
It's usually, in these times, everyone learns.
You may find, a new way will open, ahead;
(Or develop a whole, new perspective, instead.)

Don't ever fear what a challenge may bring;
Try not, to label it as 'suffering'.
Problems can often, bring times where we grow;
If we look closely- a new way may show.

Take time to breathe now, and practice self-care-
Remembering loved ones, will always, be there.
Try not to worry- please do not keep stressing;
Look closely now, for the lesson, or blessing.

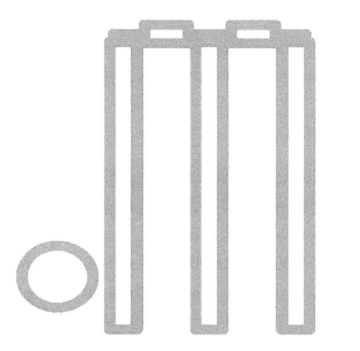

Father's Day (The Covid way)

On Father's Day;
I have to say…
I've made, a small transgression.
I didn't buy a stamp, to post your card-
That's my confession!

In fact- I didn't buy a card,
'Cos, I didn't get to the shop.
Oh dear- I'm not doing awfully well-
Perhaps, it's here, I stop!

Before I go, I'd like to say-
Just, some brief, words few-
To celebrate the man you are,
(and, just what makes you, 'you'!)

A life-long fan, of the glorious game-
(Not that one)- I mean cricket-
Well…excepting for that fated day,
When you broke your hip, on the wicket!

Contd.

Father's Day (The Covid way)

But let's move swiftly on from that-
We won't dwell on a blip!
Let's be fair- it happens to all-
A twist, a turn, a slip.

I guess, it wasn't helpful,
that you played, with broken thumb-
But hey... that's you! The show went on-
'til, you fell flat, on your ***!!

Let's leave that there... what else to say?
Ah yes- your political voice!
Your passion burns, to speak your truth-
You really have, no choice.

You know what you know, and speak as you feel-
Never sitting, on the shelf.
You are strong and steadfast...don't hold back-
Ever true, to yourself.

Contd.

Father's Day (The Covid way)

Another life-long, feature's been
a penchant, for a curry-
Which blows your head off, spicy hot!
("Can't beat a Ruby Murray!")

A love of nature, and the land;
A country boy, at heart-
Remembering tales of the riverbank,
where your young life, did start.

But wait- there's one exception-
A 'significant', at that...
You'll climb a mountain, swim a sea,
to circumvent a rat!

Otherwise, you're brave and fearless-
Independent too!
You know what you want, and what you like-
and what you like to do!

Contd.

H·A·P·P·Y
F·A·T·H·E·R·S
D·A·Y

THE ONE WHEN
WE ALL WORE
FACE MASKS

Father's Day (The Covid way)

A glass of Prosecco - always welcome!
A 'swift half' after sport-
At our house, at Christmas time-
Mince pie, with glass of Port.
(Just the one- I'm driving!)

So, the crux of this poem,
(in the absence of gift)-
Is to send you herein, to convey,
My "bestest" of wishes-
(and sorry, no card),
But, Happy Father's Day!

Happy New Year

As the Old, becomes the Past,
and the New, becomes the Now...
What thoughts run through your mind?
Who? What? Where? When? Why? and, how?

Who shared your year? (good, and bad);
What brought you joy? Or, made you sad?
What did you do, that made you smile?
When did you go the extra mile?

Why did things happen, that made you cry?
How can you live, if a loved one die?
Questions, thoughts, and life we ponder;
Wondering, what awaits us, yonder.

A time to reflect, anticipate-
Take stock, reflect, regenerate.
Has your year been easy?...
or somewhat, less than good?
Have you, struggled through with so much more,
than you ever, thought you could?

Contd.

Happy New Year

Did you eat each day?
Lie in bed at night?
Did you wake, each morn',
to see, new light?

Were there times, when you laughed,
with like- minded friends?
Were there songs to sing?
And Greetings to send?

Was there conversation, to prompt your mind?
Was a moment of humour, in each day, to find?
The year, will now soon, move into the New-
These are the things, that I wish, for you;

May you wake each day, with a heart, that's beating,
(From a restful night, of peaceful sleeping).
May your stomach be full, and your mind, be excited
At the thought of a new day - always delighted!

Contd.

Happy New Year

May you always have people, with whom you share love-
And a waterproof roof, protecting above.
May your life have true purpose, and you give more,
than get;
May many big fishes, appear in your net.

A brand, new chapter, awaiting the clock-
Some final thoughts now, whilst, still taking stock;
Smell the roses... Embrace the sun!
Use the best china... Search for 'the one'!

Be bold, be brave, stretch your soul, heart and mind;
Grab each star of happiness, there for you, to find.
Look for the good- the magnificent and true;
All things, that resonate fully, with you.

Live your life with a passion, (whatever may be);
At the end of the year, say:
"A great one for me"!

The Odd Sock

Have you stopped, and rubbed your chin,
To, ponder on this matter?
How can this keep happening?
(Illusions, now I'll shatter!)

It's often blamed on 'sock fairy'-
or sometimes, on 'House Elf,'
Or anyone who's within range,
but never, on yourself.

We often cite the washing machine,
for eating, just one sock;
But now, I'm here to tell you, that,
you really, must take stock.

There simply is no mystery -
the answer is quite clear;
Move in -listen closely,
and the truth, you now will hear!

Contd.

The Odd Sock

When you take your socks off-
You must fold them up together!
Never let them separate-
Like, bestest friends forever!

Keep them firm united,
as they journey, through the wash,
Thus, avoiding need to go and spend,
your hard-earned, dosh...

On, yet more socks, which as you know,
will go their separate ways;
Ending in the black bin bag,
that's full, of all the strays.

Grumpy

What, do you think, is just the worst,
for making you, feel grumpy?
Is it when, you slave for hours,
to find your gravy, lumpy?

What about, when you have spent an age,
on mopping floor?
Only for, a bounding dog,
to print with muddy paw.

One that really makes me cross,
is opening corned beef tin-
When key snaps off, and leaves the corned beef,
tightly wedged, therein.

A favourite gripe-
Elusive end, of sellotape that's mangled-
Thumbs and fingers ending up,
frustratingly entangled!

Contd.

Grumpy

Then the hair conditioner,
(which you grabbed with soapy eyes),
Only to get shampoo again,
(as you rub your sore, 'mince pies'.)

Maybe when you pop to shop
to get that 'vital thing' –
You get back home, and realize,
It's 'THAT'- you didn't bring!

Pen Me A Poem

WordSmith, oh WordSmith, please **write** me a rhyme,
I **need** something pronto and **just** don't have time.
My **dear** gran's 100 - a **trib**ute I want, to
Mark the occasion in **beaut**iful font.
She's a **bit** of a character - a **heap** load of fun,
And I'd **just** like to tell her "she's **my** number one".
I'll **tell** you some tales to in**clude** in my verse,
(Like the **day** that she almost be-headed her nurse).
Oh and **please** could you mention the **motor**bike fest,
When she channelled 'Hells Angel' in **black** leather vest.
And the **time** when she 'streaked' on the **pitch** at the game,
The **poor** bemused Ref has not **since** been the same.
But she's **oh** such a sweetie and I'd **so** like it marked-
(Don't **mention** the time on the **Mayor's** drive she parked).
I'd just love to give her a little keepsake, that's
Not talc or toffees, or **iced** birthday cake.

WordSmith.

Introduction to the next poem...

I have a Facebook page called 'Pen Me a Poem'.

I accept commissions through this page for 'poetry gifts', which are personalized to the recipient.

This is the 'intro. poem' on the page, featuring a '100 years old, Hell's Angel Granny'!

If I may be of help to you, with projects relating to rhyming verse, please don't hesitate to connect with me, via the page. (@penmeapoem).

I am also contactable via my website:

www.sparkle-me-spiritual.com

Amanda. x

Over to you...

I do believe that everyone
can write a rhyming verse,
It matters not what job you do-
a clerk...a judge...a nurse.

This is where, this little book,
moves into 'interactive'
Your challenge now- to write a poem,
with a 'little prize' attractive.

On the following pages,
I have given you opening line-
Your task; to choose which one appeals-
go on- you'll do just fine!

Write a poem underneath,
and choose some words that rhyme-
Then off to Facebook you can go,
to upload it, in good time.

ON YOUR MARKS...

Over to you...

A year to the date, of the launch of this book,
I will head to the page, and, take a look.
I want to encourage, people to try,
to find their 'poets wings', and fly.

Someone who uploads their writing-
Will receive a treat -exciting!
I'll choose a poem, and then I'll send-
£100 to my new, Facebook friend.

GET SET...

Over to you...

Choose a heading- I believe in you-
I know, that you can rhyme-
Just think of 'cat and hat and rat'-
Of 'time, and chime, sublime'.

You know what to do, there's time aplenty-
(It matters not, if your 80 or 20),
Have a go, and just remember-
You could win the prize, come next November!

Love,

Amanda. X

What you need to do...

On the following pages, you will find a selection of 'opening lines' for you to choose from,

Using this as 'line 1' of your poem, write a rhyming verse between 12 and 24 lines long.

Take a photograph of your poem **written in this book**, making sure all the text is clearly shown.

(You may want to write it out on rough first and then copy it into here.) If you'd prefer to type it out instead of handwriting it in here- that's fine too.

Upload your photo to my Facebook page "Pen Me a Poem" (@penmeapoem).

Please remember to 'Like' and 'Follow' the page so as you will be able to receive the notification 'tag in' if your poem is chosen as THE WINNER next year!

Extra notes...

You can enter as many times as you like, but each entry must start with a different opening line from the 4 options shown on the following pages.

There is no age restriction for entrants.

The winner will be announced next November, and the winning poet will receive £100 prize money, by 31st December 2021.

GOOD LUCK!

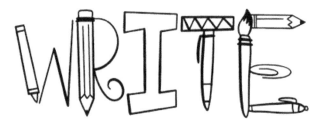

Opening line option 1

The day that I will most remember...

Opening line option 2

What do you think your mum would say...

_____

_____

_____

_____

_____

_____

_____

_____

_____

_____

_____

_____

_____

_____

Opening line option 3

If I knew then, what I know now...

Opening line option 4

There once was a planet called Earth...

_____

_____

_____

_____

_____

_____

_____

_____

_____

_____

_____

_____

_____

_____

_____

_____

_____

I am looking forward to meeting you, over on my Facebook page! (Pen Me A Poem).

Never, let anyone tell you that you can't do something, that you set your heart, on doing.

You totally CAN!

With love,

Amanda. x

Lightning Source UK Ltd.
Milton Keynes UK
UKHW021027171220
375409UK00006B/141

9 781914 133152